RSITY COLLEGE

'I HAVE A DREAM'

The story of Martin Luther King

Neil Tonge

Illustrated by Alison Astill

HODDER
Wayland

an imprint of Hodder Children's Books

Chapter 1

Martin Luther King pulled the curtain of
his hotel window to one side. He rubbed
his tired eyes with his fingers. So many
speeches. So many meetings. He had
one of the hardest jobs in the world to do,
trying to change the attitudes of
many white people towards black people.

While he was lost in his own thoughts, he caught sight of a small black boy running across the road. Tears were streaming down the boy's cheeks. His mouth was wide open in a howl of hurt and pain. Reaching the kerbside, the boy slumped down and buried his head in his hands.

What could be wrong? thought
Martin. Leaving his room, he hurried
down the staircase and walked over to
the boy.

'What's troubling you son?'

Ben looked up with wet eyes into the
face of a tall, well-built black man. His
voice was deep but it sounded gentle
and kind.

Ben didn't know where to start.
The words just tumbled out.

'We were friends.
Then they started
calling me 'blacky'.
They said they were
better 'cos they were
white. Then we scrapped.
And now we can't be
friends anymore.'

'Slow down son. Here, dry your eyes.'
Martin handed him a large handkerchief.

'What's your name?' Martin sat on the
kerbside alongside Ben as if they were the
best of friends.

'Ben. Ben Taylor Morgan.'

'Well Ben, I knew a little fella just like
you many years ago. His name was
Martin and he got into scrapes too.'

Ben stopped crying and looked straight into Martin Luther King's face.

'Was he a good fighter?' he demanded.

'Well he was at first because he got hurt just like you. Later he saw that fighting only made more people get hurt so he became a good talker instead,' explained Martin.

Ben wanted to know more. 'Tell me about him,' he said.

Chapter 2

Martin sensed that being black was different when he was six. It had been his first day at school and he was bursting to tell his friends all about it. His friends were white and they'd just started school too.

"Hold up, fella!" His mom stopped him when he got back home. "Look son, they may not want to play with you anymore."

Martin was puzzled. His mother
continued, "You've *been* friends but now...
well, just always remember you're as
good as any white person." Martin
couldn't figure this out but he
remembered what his Mom had said.

Sure enough he ended up drifting apart from his white friends. Martin began to learn quickly that black and white people were treated differently. One afternoon when he was eight he went with his father to buy a pair of shoes. A white salesman came across to them.

"I'll be happy to serve you if you'll just come to the seats in the back of the shop," the assistant said. His Dad looked the man straight in the eye. "If you don't serve us here, you won't serve us at all," he said. And with that, Martin and his father marched out of the shop.

Martin got his shoes in the end, but at a shop where they were treated with respect. That's what it was all about – treating people with respect. Many white people at the time didn't do that.

Chapter 3

As he grew older, Martin learnt that fighting always seemed to lead to more pain. It was always better to talk through a problem. At fifteen he went to college and became good at making speeches. One night when he and some college friends were returning home on a bus, the driver ordered them to get up and give their seats to some white people who were standing. "C'mon. On your feet!" bellowed the bus driver. Martin didn't like it but he did as he was told.

In the college holidays he took up jobs but always noticed that black people were paid less than white people, even when they did the same job.

Martin wasn't sure what to do when he left college. Until one day he heard Dr Benjamin Mays, the college principal, preaching about the need to change the racist attitudes of people living in the southern states of America. Martin was deeply moved by his words. He thought that preaching could help to make white and black people live closer together. That made up his mind.

In 1954, Martin became minister of the Baptist Church in Montgomery, Alabama. He was determined to persuade white people to give up their unfair treatment of black people and he wanted to do this through talking and preaching.

Then, on 1 December 1955 his life was changed forever.

Chapter 4

It turned out to be a little old lady that changed Martin's life. A tired old lady who would not stand for discrimination anymore. This lady, Rosa Parks, was ordered by a bus driver in Montgomery to give up her seat to a white passenger. She refused, nice and politely mind you, but she would not budge. In the past some black people had actually been killed for standing up for their rights. The driver didn't want to make a fuss so he called the police and poor Rosa was arrested.

In those days there were separate
seats in eating places for white and black
people, separate park benches, even
separate toilets. The other black people on
the bus did nothing. I guess they'd just
got used to discrimination or were just
plain frightened.

Well, news of Rosa's arrest spread through the black community like wildfire. Many black people had had enough of being discriminated against and there were many white people, mainly in the northern states, who supported them. The government had recently banned school segregation – separate white and black schools – after a big demonstration at a southern town called Little Rock, in Arkansas.

Many campaigners felt that a demonstration in Montgomery might help to speed up changes across the country. Martin was asked to lead the campaign. He wasn't sure at first. He'd only just arrived in Montgomery as a minister and felt that his church work should come first. Besides, he wasn't certain that black people would have the determination to carry on the campaign for many months. Finally, he was persuaded to lead the protest by the Reverend Abernathy, who later became his closest friend.

Chapter 5

First, Martin decided to hit back at the bus company. He sent out 40,000 leaflets calling on all black people to stop using the buses. This is called a 'boycott'. Black people were persuaded to share lifts in cars instead and black taxi drivers agreed to charge only the normal bus fare.

It seemed to work. When Martin drove around the city on the first day of the boycott there were only a handful of black people using the buses.

That evening he made a speech to more than 4,000 people. He said:

"We are tired of being segregated... tired of being kicked around... We have no choice but to protest. We have been amazingly patient. But we have come here tonight for freedom and justice."

The meeting agreed to continue the protest until they won and black people were no longer treated as second-class citizens.

Chapter 6

Eventually, Rosa was fined $10 and then set free, but Martin was shocked to learn how strongly some white people felt about what was going on. He received death threats through the mail and over the telephone. His father and other friends tried to persuade him not to continue as his life was in danger. Although he was afraid, Martin felt it was his duty to go back and lead the protest. One night, his house was bombed. Martin was out but his wife, Coretta and their baby daughter were lucky to escape.

Even so, Martin always wanted to forgive his attackers because he believed that violence was not the way to change people's hearts and minds. As word spread, many people from all over the world began helping his campaign. Money poured in. But Martin was afraid that once winter set in the boycott would grind to a halt, and black people would drift back to using the buses.

The bus company tried
to use the law against Martin by saying
that the boycott was illegal. When it
reached the courts it seemed as if the
protest was over. As Martin sat in the
courtroom a reporter handed him a note.
It said that the Supreme Court – the top
judges in America – had agreed that the
white people's segregation of buses was
against the law. Martin had won.

"God decided to use Montgomery as the ground for the struggle and triumph of freedom and justice in America," Martin declared to the reporter waiting outside the courtroom.

One old black lady put it more simply when she said, "It used to be my soul that was tired and my feet that was rested. Now my feet are tired but my soul is rested."

Chapter 7

'Martin was famous throughout the
world. His ideas for peaceful marches
and sit-ins and freedom songs were
copied everywhere. 25,000 people came
to hear him speak in Los Angeles, 10,000
in Chicago. In Detroit he led an amazing
40,000 marchers on a 'Freedom Walk'.'

'Martin!' A voice suddenly interrupted him. 'It's time we were on our way,' called a man from the hotel balcony.

'I'll have to go. It's been good talking to you, Ben. Remember, believe in yourself and fighting never really solved a problem.'

Martin smiled, turned and walked towards his friend who had called him. Ben got up from the kerb and watched him go.

Funny, he thought, his name was Martin too. And with that strange idea still buzzing around in his head he headed back home.

'Where've you been, Ben?' Ben's father stood with his hands on his hips and sounded angry. 'You know we're going to the meeting and we're gonna be late.' His Dad was impatient but Ben knew he would forgive him.

Some stuffy old meeting, thought Ben. This was definitely somewhere he did not want to be, but his father said it was important. So off they trudged towards the centre of Washington city.

Chapter 8

As they set off down Pennsylvania Avenue Ben's eyes grew wider and wider. Wow, he thought, the whole of America must be here, black and white. The crowds pressed in around them. Ben gripped his father's hand tightly, afraid that they might become parted.

Then, as if a signal had gone round, the huge crowd fell silent.

'What's going on, Dad? Let me see!'

Ben's Dad picked him up by the waist, swung him round and settled him on his shoulders. Ben gasped in amazement. There must be thousands of people here. More than he had ever seen in his life. Why had they all come here? he wondered.

Ben turned his head round in the direction the crowd were facing. It was then that he got a huge surprise, for the crowd's attention was focused on one black man. The very man that had talked so kindly to Ben only an hour ago.

Ben's friend, Martin Luther King, gripped the sides of the speaking desk and began his speech. The vast crowd hung on every word he said.

'I have a dream that one day
on the red hills of Georgia
the sons of former slaves and
former slave owners will be
able to sit down together at the
table of brotherhood.

'I have a dream that one day
my four little children will live
in a nation where they will not
be judged by the colour of their
skin but by the content of
their character...

'...where little black boys and little white boys will be able to join hands and walk together as brothers.

'This will be the day when all God's children will be able to sing with new meaning "Let Freedom ring!"

'When we allow freedom to ring from every hamlet, from every state and every city, we will be able to speed up that day when all God's children, black men and white men, will be able to join hands and sing in the words of the old Negro spiritual,

"Free at last, free at last.
Great God A'mighty
I'm free at last!"'

As Martin Luther King finished his
speech Ben looked around. The crowd
was silent and in some cases, tears rolled
down the cheeks of the listeners.

'It's him!' Ben shouted to his father. 'I know him!' As they walked home, Ben told his father all about the man – Martin Luther King – who had changed his life.

What happened to Martin Luther King?

One year after Martin Luther King's speech in Washington, President Lyndon Johnston invited Martin to the White House as he signed a new law – The 1964 Civil Rights Act. This banned discrimination throughout America. That same year Martin was given the Nobel Peace Prize, the highest honour in the world. Martin Luther King went on to win many more victories for black people until, tragically on 4 April 1968 he was shot and killed by a white man, James Earl Ray, who was later imprisoned.

The Civil Rights Movement did not finish with Martin's death. Since the 1960s, black people have become mayors of many towns in the southern states of America. Black representatives sit in the government of America. Many more have become lawyers, teachers, broadcasters and bankers – jobs which would have been unthinkable before. Although discrimination is against the law, it does not mean it has ended. But Martin Luther King did more than anyone else in the twentieth century to change the way people think about race and to alter the way black people are treated.

Marin Luther King (1929–1968)

Glossary

banned against the law

campaign a movement to bring about change

demonstration a gathering of people
  protesting against something

discrimination treating people differently
  because they are not the same as you
  e.g. the colour of their skin.

negro an older term used to describe black
  Africans. This term is now often considered
  offensive.

racist someone who dislikes people of
  another race

representatives people elected to act on behalf
  of groups of people in government

segregation keeping different races apart in
  schools, housing, on buses etc.